Dudley the Donkey

by Rich Lewis
illustrated by Len Epstein

Core Decodable 74

Bothell, WA • Chicago, IL • Columbus, OH • New York, NY

MHEonline.com

Copyright © 2015 McGraw-Hill Education

All rights reserved. No part of this publication may be reproduced or distributed in any form or by any means, or stored in a database or retrieval system, without the prior written consent of McGraw-Hill Education, including, but not limited to, network storage or transmission, or broadcast for distance learning.

Send all inquiries to:
McGraw-Hill Education
8787 Orion Place
Columbus, OH 43240

ISBN: 978-0-02-143359-9
MHID: 0-02-143359-3

Printed in the United States of America.

2 3 4 5 6 7 8 9 DOC 20 19 18 17 16 15

I am Dudley the donkey.
I am a jockey.

I will race Tracey the turkey.
She is a jockey, too.

Fans come to the valley to see the race.

If I am the winner, I will get fame.
I will even get a key to the city.

The fans will cheer, "Dudley! Dudley!"
The fans will toss me roses and carrots!

"Dudley! Dudley! Are you going to help with the turkeys or not?"